Dark Data and Dark Social

The Promising Problem Children of Big Data and Data Science

Lars Nielsen

New Street Communications, LLC
2014
Wickford, RI
newstreetcommunications.com

Published 2014 by
New Street Communications, LLC
Wickford, Rhode Island
newstreetcommunicaations.com

Contents

Chapter 1:
What *is* Dark Data?

Organizations that treat idle information, or so-called Dark Data, *as anything less than having potential economic benefit will find themselves at increased competitive disadvantage.*

- Douglas Laney, Gartner, Inc.

Simply put, Dark Data is stored, largely non-inventoried, unstructured data not currently used for the purpose of conducting data science, but which is nevertheless maintained on a "just in case" basis – either to meet regulatory requirements, or in the hope that the data will prove useful for research purposes at some time in the future. "Gathering dust" in archives, Dark Data, is – as less simply put by CIO and industry pundit Isaac Sacolick – "data and content that exists and is stored, but is not leveraged and analyzed for intelligence or used in forward looking decisions. It includes data that is in physical locations or formats that make analysis complex or too costly, or data that has significant data quality issues. It also includes data that is currently stored and can be connected to other data sources for analysis, but the business has not dedicated sufficient resources to analyze and leverage." Add to this unstructured data of a nature for which sufficiently robust or accurate analysis tools have not yet been invented, and some data (notably most log files) which will simply never be of use and will never yield useful Business Intelligence, commonly known as BI.

IDC estimates that approximately 90% of all Big Data is Dark Data, also sometimes known as *dusty data*.

Lurking in the labyrinth of your data cache, this unsorted, unstructured and currently un-used data generally poses not much risk from a maintenance point of view (aside from cost), but does pose security threats which must be addressed. Dark Data can easily embrace customer data which must be kept private, as well as log files and other unique, sensitive information that might be of use to hackers and/or rival enterprises.

It is essential for enterprises to balance the potential benefits from the future exploitation of Dark

Data against the threats of what such data might reveal to interlopers. By this we mean information concerning the enterprise's customer base and proprietary customer information (such as Social Security and credit card information), budgetary and P&L data, and so forth.

The great fear, of course, is that some time after an element of Dark Data is deleted or otherwise discarded, it will suddenly prove relevant to some new aspect of business development or as the solution to a previously unimagined business problem. Thus it is this nebulous potential value of Dark Data that makes us reluctant to let it go. It may be worthless, or it may be pure gold. We do not know. We have not yet drilled into it, or arrived at the currently unimaginable moment when we will need it. One is reminded of Steward Brand's old adage about *information* in general. It wants to be free, but at the same time it also wants to be expensive. The right piece of information at the right time is of infinite value, and can change everything. The exact same piece of information at another time, or in a different situation or context, is not worth a dime.

Dark Data is accumulated randomly and organically by the systems via which enterprises transact business every day. It is not data that is actively collected with any specific data science question in mind. It is the residual side effect of the functions of the enterprise – the flotsam and jetsum left over after other work is done. These include aspects of data as various as the functional records of robots at work on assembly lines (these housed in shop control systems), archived data from diagnostic devices in critical care units, point-of-sale records, phone numbers related to in-bound customer dialing, and more.

In one business such unstructured data sets as these might be of value and aggressively leveraged today – and thus not *dark* at all – while in another they might be of value only in a distant tomorrow, possibly never, and thus *very dark*. One enterprise's garbage is another enterprise's gold. "Dark" Data is "in the eye of the beholder" using both senses of the word: he or she who views it, and he or she who owns it.

Industry pundit Doug Miles sees Dark Data as having more down-side than up-side potential. He views it as something that adds further unnecessary lack of structure to already messy but genuinely valuable information, obscuring the good stuff. Miles describes Dark Data as "data that lacks any control or classification, but which is prevalent in all too many environments." Loggly's Chief Search Officer Jon Gifford sees rapidly improving storage technology tethered to increasingly efficient tools as both expanding the potential and maximizing the problem of Dark Data. "Growing application complexity and data density have been big contributing factors," he comments. "The more complex your systems are, the harder it is to identify data and discern its value. A typical system these days uses tens or hundreds of different libraries and many third party applications or services, each of which does its own thing. Staying on top of all of this is tough. The fact that storage continuously drops in price also means that you can afford to be a little less careful about how you're using it, so there is a natural tendency for data on disk to grow over time."

Like any other great enterprise benefit or potential benefit, Dark Data comes with a price: the price of storage, the price of security, and the price of a willingness to eventually develop and adopt paradigms and tools for its successful use in generating quality BI. Depending on the natures of your various kinds of Dark Data, and the situation of your enterprise, your Dark archive is a potential font of precious (indeed, invaluable) knowledge, one just waiting for the proper exploitation, the proper investment of time and tools, or quite simply for the right product and marketing problems to arise and be posed upon it, perhaps via techniques yet to be devised.

Chapter 2:
The Ebb and Flood of Data Value

Data is a precious thing, and will last longer than the systems themselves.

- Tim Berners-Lee, father of the World Wide Web

The first programming language I ever learned was Pascal – a language specifically designed, in fact, for the instruction of novice programmers. It also had its practical uses back in the day. I still have that knowledge of how to create compact, elegant code using Pascal, but what was invaluable to me thirty years ago is now worthless. With the dawn of object-oriented programming models, new and more efficient languages such as C/C++ came to the forefront. These represented completely new approaches to computer language designed for a completely new paradigm of programming. That "information" on how to program with Pascal had lost its value. It had morphed from gold to dirt. This happens all the time on a range of fronts.

But in the same place where the tide ebbs, it also floods later on. Information which might seem worthless and useless today can easily be be tomorrow's possession of great value. Isn't this the wisdom we've all used for decades to justify the hoarding of all kinds of various "junk" in our basements, attics and garages? "A minute after I throw it away, that's when I'll need it." Or so goes the familiar saying. The gimmick is that most of what we hoard we will never actually find a use for. It is unlikely the broken blade from the lawn mower you trashed five years ago will ever come in handy. On the other hand, that box of random screws will often yield some gem bound to prove essential in a particular moment. The trick is to know the difference between these items of unlikely and likely future value. This is especially the case with data, the maintenance and securing of which costs money.

The "poster child" for data that does not and probably will never have much value – often called *data debris* – is the typical log file. These are generated on every computer system running, and are quite literally logs of largely automated, trivial and redundant activities occurring on the hardware as a natural throw-off from standard operating system events and software uses, including messages between users of shared computer software. The generation of such data is organic, automatic and unavoidable. It is called *logging*. If not monitored and periodically pruned, your log files will grow like a vine in a rain forest and eat up system memory with a voracious appetite. Later on in this discussion, we'll survey specific methodologies for identifying, monitoring and deleting log files and other such data debris pests. But for now let's stick to how other, more potentially useful slices of unstructured data mature over time and become important assets.

Consider a firm which manufactures and markets widgets from coast to coast in the United States. In its early stages as a firm just starting out, it ships widgets of various shapes and sizes from just one manufacturing plant and warehouse, these located in New York. The firm's computer system maintains all sorts of transactional data related including volume purchases by customer, frequency of orders by customer, etc. - all these useful in predicting demand and thus adjusting manufacturing schedules to avoid a surplus of inventory. The system also throws off data left unstructured and unanalyzed in the moment concerning regional locations of customers – this a natural off-shoot of simply having delivery addresses on hand on the system. The regionalization of this data is, however, left untagged and unstructured.

Later on in the life-cycle of the firm, as the business grows, management decides to expand manufacturing and warehouse capacity, and to do so by adding several facilities across the country, thus minimizing the costs to deliver widgets to customers while also increasing manufacturing output.

Now, for the first time, the tagging and analysis of customer volume and behavior *by region* becomes a useful exercise. By reining in, organizing and appropriately analyzing this unstructured, previously "dark" and useless data, data scientists are able to ask questions of the data which enable decisions as to exactly where plants and warehouses should be located, and how they should be tooled. If, for example, there is greater demanded for widget *A* vs. widget *B* in the midwest than in the far west or eastern seaboards, perhaps the midwest facility should be tooled to focus primarily on the production of widget *A*. Concurrently, if there is significantly more demand in Missouri than Ohio, and these states constitute the midwest's two largest markets for your widgets, perhaps the midwest plant should be located west of the Mississippi, although not too far west.

Here is another example of how previously "dark" and unused, unstructured data can emerge from the box of random screws into the light, and be used to gain important BI.

We've all, at one time or another, called the customer service number of our insurance company or credit card company or some other service or product provider to ask a question, voice a complaint, accept a special offer, and so forth. And we've all heard the same automated voice inform us that our call may (in fact almost always *is*) recorded to assure the quality of customer service. These digital recordings are routinely archived, in large measure to provide the firm with backup should a customer deny having requested a service, or to resolve other customer disputes. (This type of Dark Data, as well as random comments expressed on Facebook news-feeds, product- and industry-specific online groups, and various other social media is usually referred to by professional data scientists as "digital exhaust.")

Many firms are now taking unstructured digital voice file data and using it to spot trends in consumer reactions, demands and complaints vis-a-vis specific products and offerings. Using voice recognition software, data scientists can search these unstructured files for key phrases – perhaps "unhappy," "annoyed," and "frustrated" – and match these in frequency with product references to reveal trends in customer satisfaction or dissatisfaction with regard to various goods and services offered by the firm. Once such files are located and isolated, they can be probed more deeply – often in a non-automated manner – by data scientists seeking BI on how to improve performance.

Chapter 3: Building a Team to Enlighten Dark Data

No discovery was ever made without a bold guess.

- Isaac Newton

Dark Data can sometimes remain dark for far too long. There can often be a need to tap a dark resource, but no clear realization on the part of management that the resource even exists, or if it exists, how to best exploit it. Data often remains dark simply because the same team or teams which have cast it aside and relegated it to unstructured purgatory in the first place are not well positioned to re-evaluate its worth later on, not equipped to consider it from a new perspective with a view toward discovering fresh business opportunities or solving emerging problems. New eyes are needed. New perspectives. New curiosity. New minds free from the assumptions and "common," accepted wisdom of the past.

What is required is that single clarity of vision possessed by people viewing a landscape for the first time – a landscape which, though boringly familiar to natives, appears full of ripe possibilities to the newcomer: the fresh and eager explorer intent on blazing new trails and making fresh, important discoveries. To mix metaphors, we need eyes which can intuitively discern precious gems hidden amid the cheap costume jewelry at the five-and-dime store.

A great scientist once said "discovery consists of looking at the same thing as everyone else and thinking something different." A great explorer once commented: "They are ill discoverers that think there is no land when they can see nothing but the sea." And I believe it was Steve Jobs who told us: "Creativity is just connecting things. When you ask creative people how they did something, they feel a little guilty because they didn't really do it, they just saw something. It seemed obvious to them after a while."

The leveraging of Dark Data requires seeing facets and possibilities which are invisible to others, envisioning possibilities which lay well beyond the obvious, and conjuring connections between disparate unstructured data sets which, though worthless standing alone, when brought together and cross-referenced yield important knowledge.

Thus you must make sure the data science team you deploy to answer BI questions with Dark Data include a careful mix of professionals. Yes, it is necessary and important to include people recruited within the organization who already know the business well, because their expertise regarding the organization's goals and business model, not to mention the institutional history of past experiments, successes and failures, is invaluable. However, as noted above, old eyes tend to look at the data terrain in the way that has become "traditional" – for lack of a better term – within the firm. Thus it is absolutely key to include fresh blood with fresh eyes and a capacity to – as the saying goes – "think outside the box" – and explore data in new ways to reveal new facts, new questions, new ideas, and hopefully, new efficiencies and profitability.

Whether these fresh eyes come in the form of new hires, or in the form of analysts and researchers from areas of a large organization where professionals have not been previously involved with the at-issue BI problem or data, or from outside consultantancies, is irrelevant. It is simply important that new blood in the form of curious, statistically-inclined programmers, analysts and modelers be a part of the mix and given license to go where their skills and intuition lead them, regardless of any pre-existing institutional biases, procedures or priorities.

Flexibility, and a willingness to accept new – and sometimes, from the standpoint of the organization, revolutionary – results, are key. "The whole point of Dark Data," says one professional, "is you don't know what's out there and what you might find. And you don't want to have too rigid a plan that boxes you into what you might end up doing." In fact, many is the time you won't even know what you are looking for until you find it. After all, that's what *discovery* is all about.

As should be clear from what I've just said, a Data Scientist is rarely ever a single person, but in fact *a team* encompassing skills ranging from programming and data cleaning, through modeling and building algorithms, to analysis. As I've made clear in my previous book – *Unicorns Among Us: Understanding the High Priests of Data Science* – these professionals are usually pulled from a range of disciplines where modelling and predictive-analysis play major roles. Here we are talking about individuals as diverse as professionals in psychology and the social sciences, political science, allied health, advanced theoretical mathematics, programming, and engineering. They rarely, if ever, come from MBA programs. Whether a programer, a modeller, or an analyst, the best recruit for a data science team is an outlier containing within him- or herself the disparate and contradictory disciplines of a strict, procedural researcher and an imaginative visionary. *In short, a very rare bird.*

At a minimum, a small data science team should include at least one software engineer and one quantitative analyst familiar with Hadoop – the Open Source computing environment most often used to wrangle unstructured data into manageable shape by preparing, integrating, cleaning, running and analyzing the unstructured information. The team should also, in my opinion, include a systems architect to maintain the systems hosting the data. Larger data science teams might include data visualization experts capable of turning results into easy-to-understand charts and graphs for management consumers of BI, and quantitively-qualified business analysts who can isolate results most valuable to the organization and effectively communicate those results in language management can understand.

But the two indispensable keys remain *curiosity* and *imagination*. When done right, studies of Dark Data should deliver new insights rather than merely confirm old insights. The new insights need not *contradict* the old; but if they don't contract the old then they should expand knowledge and provide a deeper understanding of *why* accepted wisdom should continue to be accepted, or with what nuances it should be revised. The optimal data science team will do this seamlessly, at once disrupting and enhancing the organization it serves.

Chapter 4:
The Varying Natures of Dark Data

Data is the new oil.

- Clive Humby of *dunnhumby*

Data is the new oil? No, data is the new soil.

- David McCandless

It is worthwhile to take a few moments to itemize the different types of Dark Data that might loiter in your enterprise archive, depending on the nature of your enterprise. These may include social media comments and connections, and histories regarding website and mobil transactions.

From sources like these, plus internal operations data and such things as consumer browsing histories, there is often an abundance of useful BI to be gleaned by digitally-oriented consumer-centric marketing organizations on such topics as how customers and potential customers feel about various brands, what attracts them to one offer over another, where they do their shopping, what they are looking for in a customer experience (and sometimes *exactly where* they've been disappointed or pleased), and so forth. Add to this such datapoints as sales and browsing histories associated with geolocation and mobile wallet applications.

Financial institutions likewise have a wealth of Dark Data available, should they think to look for it. Here is one example. Not long ago a major European bank began isolating and studying, for the first time, the habits of customers who dealt primarily with the institution via ATM. By wrangling the unstructured data of customer ATM transaction histories, the institution was able to isolate exactly which customers were primarily using ATMs of other institutions for their transactions instead the ATMs of their own bank. Using this data, they then used other key data points to delve into why these customers preferred competitive ATMs, and were subsequently able to customize financial products, offers and incentives to increase *direct* customer engagement.

Another type of Dark Data opportunity owned by way too many enterprises is the very darkest of Dark Data imaginable – *data so dark it is not even collected*. I recommend to all organizations that they not only explore existing undiscovered data points within their records, but also what additional data points they might easily collect going forward which might help them significantly increase their useful BI.

An example here would be a business social networking site of which I'm aware which had never thought to collect data on the simple question of whether or not their users were involved in the running of businesses primarily based on e-commerce as opposed to more traditional sales channels. By adding so small a thing as a check-box question on their enrollment questionnaire, they were subsequently able to isolate the relevant users and eventually identify a host of vital data points within that particularly defined user universe, enabling the mining of BI which came to form the basis for creating highly-profitable product offerings.

Another form of Dark Data that frequently goes not only unused but uncaptured is internal expertise within large organizations, particularly (and ironically) tech-oriented organizations. The consulting firm McKinsey tells us approximately 20% of a knowledge worker's time is spent searching for fundamental information with which he or she can do his or her job most efficiently and effectively. In other words, one entire day out of a five day working week is dedicated to isolating essential information to underpin the work of the remaining four days. Often this information is to be found in-house in the minds of colleagues, but goes undiscovered in large organizations with vastly spread out technologists, many of whom do not even know one another. Talk about unstructured Dark Data.

How to solve this problem? Microsoft came up with one solution. A few years ago, the Redmond, Washington organization launched an initiative which is best described as an "internal YouTube" upon which any employee can record his or her ideas for sharing with any other employee in the company who might be working on the same or a similar problem. More than 10,000 such videos were posted to the portal in the scope of just three years. Of course, this data would have remained quite dark, even after being put onto video, were it not for advanced Video Content Management Systems (VCMSs) which allow for the sorting and searching of video content in a manner well beyond the simple structured tag search offered by YouTube. A VCMS allows one to actually search the content inside videos by indexing every word spoken and every word displayed on screen, and even allowing viewers, once they've discovered the video or videos they need, to fast forward to the most relevant moments of the videos regarding the topics of their concern.

As should be clear by now, the range of sources for Dark Data, and the range of tools for mining Dark Data, are each abundant and growing with a speed that is hard to exagerate. In addition to taking into account the standard repositories – or perhaps we should say, "hiding places" – for Dark Data, it is vital to *imagine* in what unexpected corners of your organization, or your market, additional Dark Data might be lurking in obscurity, ripe with unrealized potential.

Creative thinking to solve a specifically defined problem is one thing, and of course very necessary in data science. But creative thinking to explore boundaries and discover hidden resources upon which *new* questions can be posed and *new answers* discovered for questions yet to be imagined, is even more important. This is where we push out the true frontiers of knowledge and genuinely discover possibilities for those products, services and profits which will contribute most dramatically to the growth of the enterprise. *This* is the fertile ground in which innovation and invention flourish.

Chapter 5:
The Need for Universal Ubiquitous Encryption

The mantra of any good security engineer is: Security is a not a product, but a process. *It's more than designing strong cryptography into a system; it's designing the entire system such that all security measures, including cryptography, work together.*

- **Bruce Schneier**, cryptographer and computer security expert

If you reveal your secrets to the wind, you should not blame the wind for revealing them to the trees.

- Kahlil Gibran

One key aspect of Dark Data, and the characteristic that makes it dark in the first place, is that for the most part we do not realize it is there, or at least to what extent is there. Or we only vaguely realize its presence and potential value. Dark Data is, as I've mentioned before, uninventoried. Securing *inventoried* data sets is a challenge, but a manageable challenge, for the enterprise. Securing uninventoried, unstructured data is even more of a challenge, but also manageable. And essential.

Just as Dark Data contains unexplored and un-evaluated prospects for data science, it also contains generally unexplored and un-evaluated potential harm should it fall into the wrong hands. It is entirely possible that your enterprise's unstructured Dark Data contains prospective data points which, if cleaned and manipulated by interlopers, would reveal current (or worse, potential future) proprietary BI that, just as it is of great value benefiting your enterprise, can just as easily be a powerful tool if deployed against your enterprise in the marketplace. This open-ended risk is the most malignant of the possible dangers of a Dark Data breach – but there are others.

First, consider regulatory and legal risks. Much Dark Data can often be information stored in order for the enterprise to be able to respond to the demands of retention regulations articulated by state and federal governments. Such Dark Data can easily include confidential credit card, bank account and other financial information. It might also include such sensitive material as the archived patient records of a health service provider. Exposure of such information might easily lead to significant financial and/or legal liability on the part of the enterprise.

Next, consider proprietary intelligence risk. Does your unstructured Dark Data incorporate information which might, if properly cleaned and studied, reveal key fundamentals of your internal budgets, business practices, competitive strategy, current or projected partnerships and/or joint ventures? Does it include information which might reveal likely plans for new products, initiatives or strategic operations? Imagine how such data, in the wrong hands, could impact important business plans, activities, and relationships. And imagine what it could do to your bottom line.

Exactly where does your Dark Data reside? How is it stored? And most importantly, how it secured? If you do not know the answers to these questions, you should.

Each and every digital asset of your enterprise, now matter how dark or how enlightened, should be safely stored under the strongest encryption, whether on premises or in the Cloud. None of your Dark Data should be open to casual browsing by anyone, even internal staff, without stiff management controls in place to guard access. And within your systems, strong PGP encryption should be structured so as to make it maximally difficult for any interlopers obtaining your encrypted Dark Data to unseal its contents. Such universal, ubiquitous encryption as this is absolutely necessary, and – astonishingly enough – too often lacking, even though such firms as Symantec, IBM, Trend Micro, Vormetric and many others offer robust, easily-installed, easily-customized and easily-maintained turnkey solutions.

In general, turnkey solutions licensed from third-parties offer significant advantages over security systems designed in-house. It is important to remember that computer security threats and computer security solutions are dynamic, constantly changing things. Skilled hackers are infinitely and tirelessly motivated to contrive ways to penetrate systems and decrypt data. Their skills and approaches constantly evolve, usually just one step behind various security solutions being deployed – if that. Thus, security solutions need to evolve as well, and security tools regularly stress-tested, refined, redesigned and strengthened. Given this, it is nearly always most economical and efficient for the enterprise to delegate these responsibilities to a third-party provider, one armed with dedicated security skills and expertise of a quality not commonly found in most enterprises.

Chapter 6:
Dark Data Retention Policies

The price of light is less than the cost of darkness.

- Arthur C. Nielsen, market researcher and Founder of *A.C. Nielsen*

It would be nice if all Dark Data could be stored endlessly and never purged. It would be great if we could always keep all options open, and know that we have the very widest of fields to prospect for important data points whenever we need to. But as mentioned previously, roughly 90% of all Big Data is Dark Data. And data in general, worldwide, is currently accumulating at a staggering rate – a rate which will only increase over time. At some point the cost of storing and securing data will force your enterprise to dispose of some information. Thus it is key that you put into place firm procedures and protocols for deciding which unstructured data stays and which goes. This, among other things, involves realistic assessment of the potential data science value held by particular data assets – a hard-nosed evaluation conducted on a precisely defined, recurring schedule.

Your data retention policy must be rigid. It also must be narrowly-defined, recognizing that there is more garbage in the can than gold, and forcing hard decisions. As tech pundit Minda Zetlin writes: "In the era of the Internet of Everything, having a broad data-retention policy – or worse no policy at all – isn't viable any longer. Machine-to machine (M2M) data traffic will have grown six-fold from 2013 levels by 2018. If all that data is retained by default, the companies doing the retaining will find themselves with a Big Data-sized problem."

Your retention policy should be defined by a team of in-house professionals which includes data scientists, systems administrators and engineers, strategic business planners, and legal counsel and compliance officers.

Data scientists can bring to the table an invaluable view as to exactly which clusters of unstructured data are most likely to yield useful BI in the future. Here we are talking about three-year-old customer comments collected through a form on your website vs. three-year-old logfiles vs. three-year-old direct-sales histories for a line of products that has since been cancelled. A well-thought-out data retention policy will, I must emphasize, put an expiration date on just about everything – setting a clock running on almost every piece of data your organization possesses. However, the more potentially useful and vital the data, the longer the clock can and should be set for. It is here the data scientist is in the best position to make judgements and recommendations as to different classes and types of unstructured data.

Systems administrators and engineers bring to the table an acute sense of the realistic capabilities to archive data, always with a keen eye on the expenses related to the storage and securing of the data. It is for the systems administrators and engineers to make clear the realistic capacity of existing resources, the attendant costs, and the costs that might be associated with expanding that capacity, should such a decision be in the wind. In most organizations, systems administrators and engineers are often somewhat at odds with data science teams, as the latter are chiefly concerned with swimming and playing in as large a pool as possible, while the former are concerned with maintaining and paying for the pool, and have an interest in making sure it stays as small as possible. This creative tension, however, usually results in a good balance between "the demand" and "the possible." In this environment, data scientists are forced to concede some thoughtful strategic pruning of their raw material, while systems staff are forced to justify any real or conceived constraints on data storage.

Business strategists bring to the table a more "structured" – if you will – vision of what the future of the enterprise might be than do the visionary data scientists. While the data scientist will be – *and should be* – concerned with having data with which to discover the previously unimagined, the business strategist will be concerned with maintaining data of a type most likely to be of use in advancing some predefined and established business plan, such as a specific new group of products already in development, an expansion to another region or country, or a corporate rebranding agenda.

Legal counsel and compliance officers bring to the table a concern for maintaining any data which might potentially be needed in current or anticipated litigation. These professionals also bring to the table a knowledge of exactly which data must be maintained in order to meet federal and/or state data retention mandates and conform with all related laws and regulations. And perhaps most importantly, it is legal counsel and compliance officers who can say exactly when mandatory data can be deleted without federal or state blowback.

Through shared analysis, discussion and compromise, this group should define the enterprises's data retention policy. The data retention policy, meanwhile, should be reviewed and revised at least once a year by the same group, to make sure it evolves with the dynamic priorities and needs of the firm.

In very rare instances, there will be some types of data which should never be assigned a so-called "end-of-life" or "sundown" date, and should be retained permanently. But if this represents 5% of your enterprise's archived information, it'll be a lot. And your data retention committee must decide which data this is – as it'll vary greatly from enterprise to enterprise.

According to an Applied Research report: "Almost 90% of IT and legal pros value data retention plans, but less than half their organizations have them and many fail to follow through with required technology." According to Dan Milrad, a senior manager at Symantec: "There's definitely a gap in terms of what people perceive as important around information management – around retention policies, deletion policies – and what their actual practices are." But, says industry-pundit Matthew J. Schwartz, such plans, and dedicated follow-through on those plans, are essential in order to avoid an inefficient and costly "pack-rat" approach to data storage, especially as regards Dark Data.

In general, "data debris" of the types which are readily disposable by most firms include short-term reference files, orphaned files, outdated files, safety and litigation copies related to systems upgrades, out-of-date storage technology, and technical duplicates.

With regard to short-term reference files, it is important to remember that most dumps, logs, and automated reports from database systems and apps lose their value rather quickly. Also, many project teams are guilty of leaving behind useless work files at the end of a development endeavor. All such information as this should be routinely scrutinized as candidates for disposal.

With regard to orphaned files, we are talking here about non-essential data regarding former employees. We are also talking about misfiled or mislabeled data (such as data not conforming to recently adopted standards in naming) which will thus become invisible in your systems though nevertheless continue to eat up storage capacity all the same. And we are talking about files deriving from abandoned applications, and useful only in relation to those abandoned apps.

With regard to superseded, outdated files, examples here would include early versions of later finalized drafts of analysis, or abandoned analyses. Here we are also talking about the previous "working versions" of any and all documents subsequently finalized.

With regard to safety and litigation copies of files related to systems upgrades, here we are talking about a particularly storage-hungry type of beast. During system upgrades and/or replacements, the process of merging data files with the new systems nearly always causes massive duplication, not to mention the intentional creation of "safety" copies of data files that are often eventually forgotten rather than disposed of. As regards data files retained for use in likely litigation, these are often forgotten once the litigation resolves itself, and can often represent many terrabytes of useless, redundant and/or superfluous information.

With regard to outdated storage technology, it is key to keep in mind that not only does data "grow hair," but so do storage systems themselves. Look into all your legacy systems and you're almost sure to find a vast clutter of digital debris.

With regard to technical duplicates, note that most experts estimate that only about 15% of automatically generated duplicate files are necessary for the maintenance of system integrity and the value of related data. Such essential duplicates might, depending on your enterprise's needs, include backup documentation related to files elsewhere in the system, configuration files for databases, as well as – from a non-technical point of view – files maintained for purposes of litigation or in accordance with accounting rules or state or federal guidelines. But the remaining 85% can and should be seriously surveyed with an eye toward deletion.

Chapter 7:

The Safe Disposal of Data Debris via Crypto-Shredding and Other Approaches

War is ninety percent information.

- Napoleon Bonaparte

Back in the old *Mad Men* days, the way to safely and securely dispose of unwanted but nevertheless sensitive files involved paper-shredding followed by burning. When conducted in bulk, it meant the use of very large industrial shredders, followed by deposit of the shreds into a furnace. The goal was, of course, the total irrevocable annihilation of information. The mission was to make the files extinct – equally as absent as the T-Rex. (Of course, we've all also seen dozens of films wherein crazed and nervous white-collar felons, with the Feds hot on their paper-trails, frantically shred items that might be used as evidence against them. The goal is not only to remove the data from your storage, but to make sure no-one else can ever lay hands on it.)

For many years now, the digital media equivalent of shredding and burning paper files has been the erasure and/or destruction of local on-premises drives. This has been accomplished generally by the over-writing (rather than the mere deleting) of files, degaussing (which erases the magnetic field of various storage media), and physical destruction by disk shredding and other means.

All of these tasks have, since the dawn of business computing until recently, been the standard approach to on-site data destruction. But with the rise of cloud computing and big data, new tools and approaches have emerged along with new problems and new issues, not the least the massive amount of files that need to be sorted and dispatched to digital oblivion.

For any of the legion of enterprises who now use cloud services to store and process their data, there is necessarily a very real concern regarding how to absolutely guarantee stored cloud data is totally and irrevocably deleted once the decision has been made to do so. Fact is, many of the features that make the cloud a "secure" and "safe" place for data in the first place also make it insecure when it comes to the the proper elimination of data. Routine cloud backups designed to assure the constant availability and integrity of data make it very hard to say, on any given occasion, that data which has technically been "destroyed" is not actually available and recoverable *somewhere* in the digital space. Further complicating matters is the possibility that your cloud provider's data infrastructure may not fully support your particular data destruction requirements. Thus, destruction of sensitive data in the cloud is awash in uncertainty.

However, we do have some options.

One popular approach to destroying data in the cloud is called *crypto-shredding*. This paradigm calls for the destruction of each and every encryption key. To make the key absolutely unrecoverable, systems administrators rotate them for active storage and then shred. Of course, all archival data is effectively obliterated once the key no longer exists. However, this strategy is only possible if your cloud provider's infrastructure allows for the rotation of keys and guaranteed deletion.

A popular approach for locally held files is Disk/Free space wiping, this often combined with physical destruction. Here we are talking about overwriting data with random patterns, then the degaussing or the employment of strong magnets to scramble hard drives in such a way that data becomes impossible to recover. In some cases, firms will go a step further by destroying the physical storage media and/or shredding magnetic media, even though this is not really necessary. After the scrambling of hard drives, the data is as permanently gone as the Dodo Bird – assuming it has not been backed-up or archived elsewhere. But note that the process of overwriting can take a very long time, depending on the capacity of the media.

A final step vis-a-vis cloud environments is to use content discovery tools to make sure the "destroyed" and "irretrievable" data does not in fact hover in duplicate elsewhere in the cloud. That such duplicates do in fact exist is almost inevitable, given the fact that secure backups are one of the major benefits offered by the cloud paradigm in the first place. Wherever redundancy is found, all steps of destruction must be repeated.

Of course, the varying tools, procedures and protocols for data destruction embraced by varying cloud service providers, and the differences in infrastructure capabilities between service providers with regard to data destruction, should be key considerations in your enterprise's choice of providers. *Make sure your provider's capabilities and policies match your needs.* Further, your Service Level Agreement with your provider *must* precisely articulate procedures for secure data destruction, leaving nothing to the imagination. Randomness is not our friend.

It is important, of course, to maintain records of destroyed data – what the information was, and precisely when and how it was destroyed – for compliance purposes. Such records are essential.

Chapter 8:

Summing Up: Recognizing the Value Within Non-Transactional Dark Data and Exploiting "Dark Social"

The number one benefit of information technology is that it empowers people to do what they want to do. It lets people be creative. It lets people be productive. It lets people learn things they didn't think they could learn before, and so in a sense it is all about potential.

- Steve Ballmer

The value of transactional data – nearly all of this structured – is neither obtuse nor abstract. The relevance of customer addresses, credit card data, purchasing histories, etc., is plain. But it requires *imagination* to recognize the information-value which hides within the unstructured data darkness; it takes foresight to discern and seperate data debris from potentially precious informational gems.

Thus it is vital for data scientists to be able to *envision relationships* between various nuggets of seemingly-unrelated unstructured data, pieces of data which alone may yield absolutely no useful BI, but which taken together can prove a rich source of actionable knowledge. As Neo Technology CEO Emil Elfrin notes: "While it can appear obscure and unhelpful, if approached in the correct way, Dark Data can reveal all kinds of patterns and insights that would otherwise have been missed. In short, it is information that can really make a difference if interpreted correctly."

The information yielded can vary from key marketing intelligence to methods for improving employee relations within the firm. One useful example of the latter can be found in the story of an airline catering firm based out of Chicago's O'Hare Airport. Puzzling over a very high 50% annual attrition rate amongst its more than 1000 employees, a data scientist commissioned by the firm was able to triangulate Dark Data on attrition, compensation, demographics, and transportation options to show that attrition was directly related not to salaries, but to distance between the airport and employee places of residence, and the transportation options connected to those places of residence. Travel logistics and residential geography hence became factors in the hiring process, and attrition was reduced to 13.5%. All the data used was existing Dark Data which, when illuminated in unison, revealed a discernable pattern.

As is so often the case, for-profit enterprises are a few steps ahead of other enterprises, such as educational and healthcare institutions and other non-profits, in recognizing the inherent value of Dark Data. As Melissa McCormack, Research Manager at Software Advice, has noted: "For-profit businesses tend to see the value of Dark Data right away, whereas it's less obvious or immediate for the nonprofit sector. But imagine if [the educational and healthcare sectors] were mirrored after the customer service or financial service industries in regards to the way they use data to make businesses decisions. The potential to service students and patients in the manner in which the consumer and financial services pursue their target population is huge. So much paperwork is involved in both education and academics, so the data is there – and in the age of electronic health records government incentives, much of it in the healthcare space is now digital. However, it needs to be mined and analyzed in order to lead to opportunities that effect the change which usually results from the strategic use of personal and behavioral data."

For our purposes, let's put the emphasis on behavioral data for this, in the opinion of most practitioners, is the real "meat" of the potential value of Dark Data. In some instances, organizations engaged in online marketing have been able to mine terrific business intelligence not from looking strictly at units of specific products moved, or price elasticity, but rather consumer behavior and volume as matched against time of day or day of week. In other instances, organizations involved in cold-call prospecting for clients have, by comparing percentage of positive responses against time of day and extrapolating upon this information through predictive analytics, been able to optimize the staffing of call-centers to match those time periods which prove statistically to be most successful.

Despite the increasing necessity for its use, the art of Data Science remains a very slippery thing to define. Josh Bloom, lead principal investigator at the UC Berkeley Institute for Data Science (BIDS), characterizes the discipline as "a context-dependent way of thinking about and working around data – a set of skills derived from statistics, computer science, and physical and social sciences." Cathryn Carson, an associate dean of Social Science at the same institution who is heavily involved with the school's Social Science Data Laboratory (D-Lab) calls Data Science "a kind of social engineering. I don't even know the ontology to describe it with. It's not a discipline; it's not a branch of science; it's a platform for building a coalition. It's one of these interdisciplinary, non-disciplinary spaces where people get stuff done in interesting ways, but don't even know what to call it themselves."

Whatever the precise definition – if there indeed is any such thing – the Data Scientist is the key to discerning what of Dark Data is usable and essential, and what is debris. In today's competitive business environment, enterprises can leave no advantage unexplored or unexploited – most particularly, in many cases, the potentially invaluable insights to be gleaned from the proper configuration, contextualizing and study of Dark Data – often a daunting but nevertheless necessary task.

"Different types of analysis present varying degrees of complexity" writes industry analyst John Rossi. "Generally speaking, descriptive analytics like social media sentiment analysis, which provides insight into what has happened, are relatively easy to do. However, diagnostic analytics, which provides insights into why it happened, predictive analytics, which provides insights into what will happen, and prescriptive analytics, which provides insights into how businesses can make something happen, are increasingly complex to conduct."

In part because of this complexity, and in part because of a "fear of the unknown" or "fear of the dark," many enterprises do not explore or exploit Dark Data at all. "People don't want to take responsibility for [Dark Data] themselves and don't know where to start," comments Doug Miles, director of AIIM Market Intelligence. "But those who are starting to deal with it are seeing huge benefits and there is a huge market opportunity ..." Miles goes on to emphasize the necessity for enterprises, as a first-step, to "re-energise" their existing ECM installations, remove silos, and link legacy systems in order to get their Dark Data "pre-conditioned" and a bit more searchable. As with everything else worth doing, we must start with the basics and re-invent the fundamentals of managing the life-cycle of data from the day of its inception.

But it is also important to realize that not all Dark Data has gray hair. Much data is technically "dark" the moment it is born. Consider, if you will, the vast volume of unstructured data generated every day through action on the personal digital devices of individual consumers constantly communicating, shopping and sharing. All this activity on all these gadgets creates countless digital footprints – footprints which if properly isolated and exploited can empower marketers to gain a far better understanding of their customer base and serve them key messages and offers at scale. This data is generally referred to as "Dark Social" – a term coined by former *Atlantic* Senior Editor Alexis C. Madrigal.

Usually, when we talk about digital sharing of photos, posts, videos, etc., we speak of the common social networks such as Twitter and Facebook. But in fact these networks represent only a small percentage of the social sharing that is transacted online every day. It is vital for marketers to also harvest and exploit the vast Dark Social which manifests variously in e-mail, IM traffic, and chat sessions, as well as posts to forums and other esoteric digital spaces.

Dark Social – if exploited with expertise and vision – offers great and too-frequently untapped advantages and opportunities for targeting, servicing and growing customer bases. Major bluechip media companies such as Universial Music Group, Universal Pictures, IPC Media, and talkSPORT have led the way in mastering and using Dark Social to illuminate their markets, with other firms close on their heels.

With regard to the rising importance of Dark Social, we have to understand the rapid decline of *direct* traffic to specific web sites, versus the flow to these sites via largely anonymous referral agents (chats, etc.) Consider, for example, the web site of the *New York Times*. Over a two year period, the *Times* lost a whopping 80 million direct homepage visitors. This number represents about 50% of the total visitations previously. The demise of *direct* visits to this and other homepages across the web shows how homepage content – whether media content such as that offered by the *Times* or other content – is no longer a precise, deliberate destination for consumers who type in the page's URL or click on a direct bookmark. Rather, *the consumer has become the destination for the content.* News and other data "find" the consumer via Dark Social referral agents – be these newsgroups, chat-boards, IM communications, chat apps or direct e-mails. This results in the consumer accessing homepage content through a roundabout rather than direct route.

A 2014 study by the online advertising firm RadiumOne found that: "Sharing activity through email, instant messaging and forum posts, *aka* Dark Social, is three times larger than the sharing activity on Facebook, globally. 69% of all sharing activity takes place via Dark Social globally versus 23% via Facebook." In other words, data science research which excludes Dark Social is missing two-thirds of the available data – those clicks to a website which come through largely anonymous referrals: unspecified and undefined social "shares." But we of course can count on this changing over time as organizations and enterprises continue to seek out every and any competitive advantage they can find.

"There's a big world of sharing going on out there which is not being dictated by social media," says RadiumOne's Kerry McCabe. "Across the 260,000 large global sites in our network, we see at least 60 per cent – sometimes 80 per cent – of all sharing happening with old-school copy and paste links or articles, which are sent via email to the people who really matter in someone's network. There's nothing really intimate or relevant about blasting your whole social network with something that's relevant to an important but much smaller group of people who really matter."

Thus Dark Social has begun to rise as a major factor in data science research and experimentation. Isolating and tracking "off the grid" referral sources will prove more and more critical to marketers and publishers as time goes on.

*

In this little book I have endeavored to explain the rudiments of all aspects of Dark Data, and to do so in language understandable by lay people: those executives and marketers and publishers who increasingly rely on data science to reveal actionable BI, but who are not themselves technical leads in their enterprises.

Dark Data is in many ways a mysterious and contrary thing – both a threat and an asset, both a cave packed with useless bits of information and a rich store house of valuable knowledge just waiting to be discovered, recovered and exposed to the light of day.

As has been shown, to separate the fool's gold from the real nuggets, and to strategically query those unstructured nuggets in a profitable manner, takes not so much science as it does intuition, imagination and inspiration. It also takes a management which is willing to invest the time, effort and dollars necessary to build an effective data science team and empower them to productively explore the undefined and unstructured information landscapes contained within both current and legacy systems, and as well investigate Dark Social elements as they relate to the specific enterprise.

About the Author

Lars Nielsen is a highly respected systems analyst and developer living in Amsterdam. His books include *Unicorns Among Us: Understanding the High Priests of Data Science, Computing: A Business History,* and *A Simple Introduction to Data Science.*

Made in the USA
Monee, IL
04 November 2026

67377629R00036